A Misfit's Ruminations

Apoorva Ravi

BookLeaf Publishing

India | USA | UK

Presentation by *BookLeaf Publishing*

Web: www.bookleafpub.com

E-mail: info@bookleafpub.com

ISBN: 9789360942793

First edition 2024

*I dedicate this book to the questioning mind in
each one of you.*

ACKNOWLEDGEMENT

I am grateful to all the people, conversations and events that inspire me to write.

Table of Contents

What if the river doesn't want to meet the ocean?

The river has no choice but to be one with the ocean and accept the unknown...
But in fact the river does have a choice,
What if she goes underground?
What if she chooses to dry up before reaching the ocean?
What if someone gave her shelter and built a dam, till she feels alright to join the ocean?

If the river is a child,
And the ocean, the outside world,
Doesn't the child have a choice to relate to the world, at its own time and manner?
Is it necessary to subject a young mind
to a harsh competitive world,
In the name of justifying the worldly evils?
Why can't we save the child?
And nurture it till it's ready,

Ready not when we feel it,
But when the child opens the key to the dam
willingly...

Who was she?

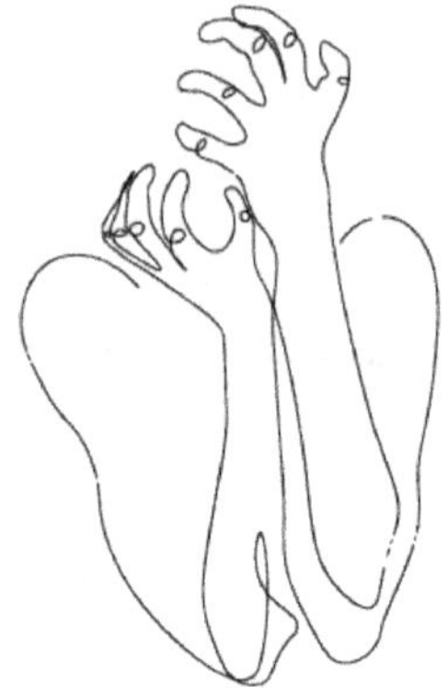

She cried aloud, in the hospital
Who was she? Who cried and made her parents
happy?
She was a newborn girl.

She cried aloud at the goldsmith shop
Who was she? Who cried and made the society
happy?
She was a girl who had just got her ears pierced.

She cried aloud in the bathroom,
she was shocked, blood was dripping from her
body!
Who was she?
Who cried, but society worried not about her
cries,

but covered up the blood stains formed every
month?
She is a woman, society said, and not a girl
anymore...

Next when she cried, no one knew why...
So they tried to stifle her cries...
But she knew, she had to cry louder...
She had to cry louder to be heard

They still didn't know why she cried...
She after all had everything—a family, job and
children
Everything that a woman wants to be—
a wife, a mother and a working woman

She had it all..
Yet she cried!
And no one knew why...
Only she knew,
She cried because
She was not only a woman, wife, mother or
working woman;
She cried helplessly, because
Everyone had forgotten that she was also a
human,
Crying for help...

She

A silent dove or a vocal lark—she may be both,
or none.
But, the world is not aware …
Or maybe does not care?
Of the innocence reflected in every talk,
The simplicity in her walk...

They hear not when she cries,
They care not when she tries…
To make everything right
Or trying too hard to delight…

She is too difficult, said some,
She is as plain as paper, said the other
Perhaps she was both, perhaps none…

This is what she thinks, this is what she feels

But it's sad that she's not aware…
That the world rejoices her laughter
And always wipes her glistening tears.
But she is not aware, let us make her aware...

I heard them today

(Context: The poem is in response to the celebrations of masses who do not think about others.)

I heard them today,
I heard them shout,
Friends, relatives, acquaintances and society,
I heard them echo their voice loudly
That they diminished any other voice out there...
Was it right?
That they thought that only their voice matters?
That they showcase their ownership over trivial
things with such force,
Forgetting that they are but transient beings on
this earth...
Forgetting that they are humans first like
everyone else...
Forgetting that there are others who might not
understand what they are saying...
Forgetting that they need to accept differences,
They celebrate something so trivial

Forgetting the real world that exists outside their bubble...

8

I am not as fickle as you say

I am not fickle as you say,
I am not unreliable as you think,
I have found my pathway through my choices
even when it seemed that I may sink...
By choosing to leave some options
I now have a better life situation,
By choosing to have diverse experiences
I now have a diverse background,
I don't question you,
So why do you question my choices?

My choices have shaped me,
And I own it with pride...
Don't tell me they are wrong,
Because both you and I know,
There's nothing right or wrong...
I don't question your consistency
So why do you question my free spirited
personality?

Why not just understand,
That I am me and you are you?

10

Choice

Why is a choice so important?
Why can't you just comply?
I don't work that way, I said
Oh you are rebellious, they said from their
position of institutional power
You are stubborn, they said, you are not a good
girl,
Now as I think about it
Why is it important to have a choice?
Why is it important to question?
And not take the pill of obedience?
Choice is important!
And more importantly, it is essential for choice
to be respected
Have you ever imagined being stripped of your
choice?
That's how I felt when you, being my teacher,
chose to lie,

When you chose to hide,
When you chose to act,
In the name of my well-being,
When you instigated me, when I was holding on
to my choice,
In the name of societal and institutional norms...
First you bated me to make that choice,
And then you took that choice away?
Why?
Why did you think it was legitimate
To take decisions on my behalf
Why did you think it was right to go behind my
back?
I am posing this question,
Trying to appeal to your conscience
But I forget that you have none left!!

I look at the mirror

I now look at the mirror and smile
Since I feel like I have come alive...
With a sense of realisation that
enveloped me,
Like something just clicked within me,
For now I have the answers to my burgeoning
questions,
That I am different and on the spectrum...
But it's not a badge of fashion,
It's just me having made sense of my actions,
Without hope of any gain or accommodation,
It's just me trying to understand
What's within me,
So that I can relate better with
what's outside of me...

My instinct is not a delusion

Yes, my thoughts are valid to me
My perceptions are valid, even if you call it an
assumption or perhaps a delusion?
For it's not just a delusion but an instinct I can't
ignore...
It's an instinct I need to explore...
Perhaps there are some aspects of this instinct
that are redundant and I need to let go...
But there are some aspects of the instinct I need
to embrace in steps if not in one go...
Because it's the same instinct that helped me
develop a sense of trust with the self...

But you come along, in your white coat and
prescription pad,
And tell me that all my thoughts are wrong and
invalid,
That they are delusions and can't be trusted or
valid,

You told me and the world that I can't be trusted
and need to be medicated?
Why? Why can't you care for my thoughts
instead?
Why can't you just listen and let them trickle
down...
Whether it's a delusion or hallucination, it will
fade with time
as I heal with love and listening...
For let me tell you when I had that delusion and
hallucination
It was my mind crying for care and attention
But you oh smiling white coat,
Shut me up with diagnosis and medication!

But now I have awoken,
I trust my voice
I am slowly rebuilding my sense of self
Without the help of you in the white coat
Because, I was fortunate that there were others
who listened...
Others who care,
And aid me develop a sense of self,
Where I co-create myself by relying on the self.

Presence of the present

Nature stood silent,
As I passed by her, gently swaying now and
then,
She synced her movement to the pace of my
body,
As I walked on the terrace...
The smell of flowers,
The flutter of leaves,
The crickety insects,
Drew me inside...
Taking me away from the past or the future,
And bathed me with the headiness of the
presence of the present...
I stopped going back or forward,
And just paused in the present.
For it's all I have,
For it's all we have
For today is beautiful when relished today
Not tomorrow or yesterday...

Love is Good, Bad and Ugly

Love is Good, Bad and Ugly
I realise that now,
having experienced it firsthand...
I can tell the difference about when it's a
connection and when it is a mere obsession,
I now value the look in your eye, when it used to
flirt with my face...
I now value the silly conversations, between
Silent pauses, when I was wondering what's
going on in your head...
I now value the nakedness of each other than the
artifice of societal clothing,
I value the urgency to be together
and not the pressure to be bounded together...
I want to value you, as much as I value me
But I think that's an infinite aspiration below
which we mortals survive
and just hope to thrive...

Eyes Wide Open

I looked at them,
I peered into their eyes and smiled
I didn't get scared this time,
And I thought back of a time when I would enter
a room looking at the ground...
Was it social anxiety?
Perhaps,
But why label?
It was just a fear of the unknown...
The unknown was something I had learned to be
afraid of...
Not knowing whether it would be a delicious
pizza
Or a bottle filled to the brim with bitter gourd
juice?

I now wonder, what if it could be both or
perhaps none?
It's life sweetheart, I tell myself now
Whatever it is,
It needs to be enjoyed with eyes wide open!

A permanent fixture

Looking at you, look at me,
Is now a distant memory...
I remember the traces of your touch
On my hand,

Now as I think of
The definition of love,
Only you come to my mind

I am trying hard to let go,
Of you, oh my! Oh love!
But you have captured my soul
Body and mind

As I turn the pages back, honey
Of our loving memories
I see a shared bond
That tended our love

But now it's over you say
Ignore my calls and message
Are we not even friends in your mind?

I just want to know honey
If you are happy and healthy
Why don't you let me inside?
Your mind?

I don't have any expectations,
Of a future together
All I want for you,
Is to be happy
But you will always be
A permanent fixture in my mind

I am not a child

Look at me, I am not a child
Don't think, I can't decipher the broken pieces of
the puzzle...
That engulfed me...
You didn't trust me, to tell me what's wrong
Don't hide under the pretext of right and wrong,
Social norms are but a reason to shut me up...
You know what happened,
Don't play the role of a gullible soul,
You didn't ask how I felt, or try to listen to my
side of the story,
When you labelled me...
You were aware of my grief, when you took
away my agency,
Now things have changed,
I have reclaimed my agency
Now I am aware,
Aware of my emotions,
And trying to heal, by making sense of them,

I am hopeful of a tomorrow with healthy
boundaries,
Of nurturing relationships with friends and
family,
With care and mutual respect
And not fear and mistrust
That breeds suspiciousness, lies and distrust...

Let the ice cream melt

Let the ice cream melt, honey,
It's all right, I like the milkshake...
Let the smoke fill the air, don't open the window,
Darling, let's inhale it in together, the
intoxication of each other,
Let's fill the night with our memories together
It's our night, let the silence speak
As we sway to the tunes of our unique rhythm,
That's music to only our ears,
A lullaby that lulls us to sleep in each other's
arms...
My love, let's drown in the abyss of each other's
warmth...

A trail of unforgettable memories

Some take time to be a part of us,
Some we take a liking to immediately,
Some we want with us all the time...
And some, for certain bursts of time.
Aren't the songs we listen to similar?
Aren't the people in our lives similar too?
We meet, we greet, hold onto some, some more
closer than others, bid goodbye to some others…
But each one leaves something behind
A trail of unforgettable memories...

Stumble, Fumble and Crumble

Stumbling, with my foot dangling from the
pathway of expectations,
I struggled, yet marched ahead...
But it was not easy,
I was fumbling, scared of conversations
Still I managed to get a few words
right in front of you all...
With the uncertain fear,
that the wrong words would leave me an
outcast....
But I tried to stay afloat.
Still, I was crumbling under the pressure of it
all...
Why do we all stumble, fumble and finally
crumble?
When nothing matters but today?
But like always, the sun overshined and the
moon hid
No one is happy, not the sun nor the moon

But perhaps happiness is a mythical term
That's trying hard to find the fine balance between
Stumble, fumble and crumble...

Beauty outside my backyard

Tinted with water droplets, my spectacles
showed me the beauty outside my backyard,
The rain created an envelope of softness and
surrealness
As it's coolness kissed my lips
The sitar music playing through my mobile
stereo
Synced perfectly with the sound of water
droplets
Creating an imagery worth capturing...
Which me and my cat watched, mesmerised and
awestruck,
It's like we were squeezing out the most from
this moment,
All the wonder and joy that it could offer,

Like two tiny kids slurping the last part of the
lollipop,
while walking home,
Sharing their day with each other and their
mothers.

My Mental Health Concern

I think of it as a struggle sometimes,
And sometimes as an entity around which the
stigma has to be broken,
I often looked at it from other people's lens and
felt misunderstood...
But nowadays I ask myself...
It's not bad, isn't it?
My mental health concern with its medium highs
and lows,
Is a part of me...
A part that has shaped my empathy,
A part that has shaped my open attitude to life,
A part that has shaped my inner light,
A part that craves to be understood,
A part that loves to be loved,
A part that loves animals fiercely,
A part that's curious about human beings,
A part that loves to share,
Stories that hope to be understood!

Yes I am a jigsaw puzzle
With my mental health concern being an
irreplaceable piece!

Where did you hide this smile?

Hiding...
Trying to keep it under wraps
I try hard...
But why is it so difficult?
To keep things to myself?
I tried hard yesterday,
I tried hard today,
And failed miserably...
Why?

Why do I want to always reflect my emotions on
my face?
I schooled my nerves to keep calm!
Remain unflinching,
But they betrayed me!
The nerves...
They tried to nudge my face muscles into a
smile...
I resisted,
But in wane...
I then smiled!
I smiled at the world outside,
Smiled with all my heart.

Oh where did you hide this smile for so long?

They said.
Little did they know,
That their sarcasm,
Their callousness,
Their ridicule,
Had made me wish my smile away
But now I will not let my fear of their censure
Swallow me or my smile anymore!

The Cold Water

The cold water crept slowly,
And softly caressed my toes…
The water gave me time to get used to the
coldness…
Helping me come to terms with it,
Starting from being cool, then mildly cold, to the
harsh chilly cold,
The water, she showed me the complete
spectrum of coldness, that some relationships
offer just before,
They freeze and do not flow anymore.

You are a big deal

When you feel the walk is much longer and the
destination obscure,
Remember, you are a big deal
When you feel that how much ever you do, you
are not seen;
Remember, you are a big deal
When the scars of the past, haunt your morning
dreams;
Remember, you are a big deal
When the doubts of tomorrow, keep you up at
night;
Remember, you are a big deal
When everything you do, falls crashing down;
Remember, you are a big deal
When you can't match up to society's
expectations,
Remember, you are a big deal
When you are touted as too sensitive and too
complicated,
Remember, you are a big deal

When you are measured against the 'so called
normal standards',
Remember, you are a big deal
When nobody remembers your name,
You remember, you are a big deal
When you don't remember anybody's name,
Remember yours, because you are a big deal!

My Love

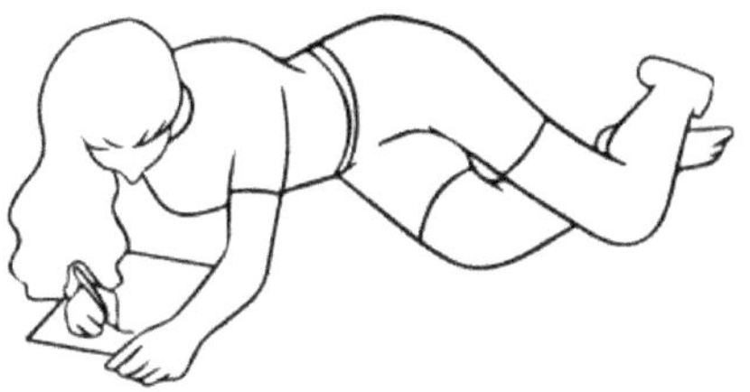

The emotion that I experience for you love, is
true,
I want to hold you,
And let you hold me, in an embrace of two,
I want to love you at this moment with all my
intensity,
But love, tomorrow it will all be too good to be
true…
I do not feel the same way everyday,
I am like the river flowing,
And changing from day to day,
You think I love you infinitely
But no, my dear one, my love for you is
time-bound,
Like the sand trickling down the sand clock,
My love for you trickles down...
And the more you try to hold me,
I run away like the sand,
That escapes from between your fingers,
The more you try to hold me,
The far I run, leaving you way behind...

Letter To My Lover

You entered my space,
You intersected with my thoughts—
Poured your emotions into my melting pot
Which, I devoured willingly…
We tried to be a version of ourselves that would
appeal to the other.
But we failed...
We failed to reach the midpoint
We broke up and patched up multiple times…
With each fall and rise, I was introduced to a
different facet of you and you to mine…
You saw me for what I am—a set of broken
glass pieces…
I saw you for what you are—wounded...
I wanted to try to understand...
I wanted to help you heal…
But you refused to pick the broken pieces of my
soul…

The Parting

I am tired, he said
And I knew that the end was near.
The end of a period that felt like a roller coaster
ride...
A period of bittersweet memories…
End of a journey of friendship and
understanding...
Alas! I wish it could have remained that way
But the expectations were there from both
ends...
Expectations that became bigger than us…

Free Bird

I wish I could quit my job today and travel
everywhere…
Where people would not question me
Whenever I go here and there…
I would roam around the earth like a free bird
With no one at my lair..
But alas the new norm has different plans!
I did not go anywhere
I did not quit my job…
But got laid off, out of nowhere!
I can travel but with caution
With sanitizer and temperature checks
everywhere…
Pub, cafe and parks—every place has a
checkpoint of beeping thermometer and
oximeter…
I wished I could be a free bird…
But I am nothing but a masked bird,
With doctors and BBMP always at my lair!

I have come a long way

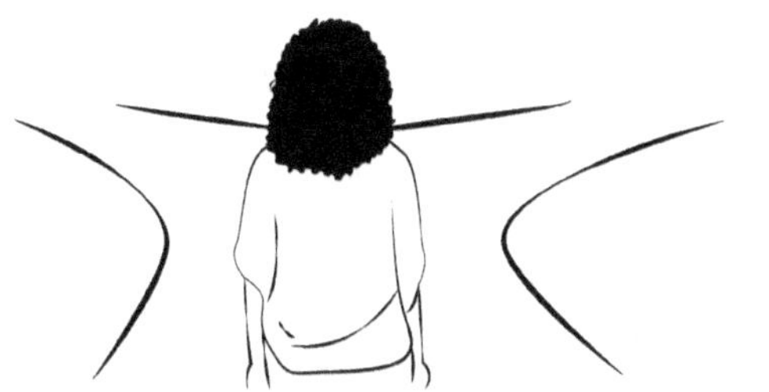

From being scared about what others will say…
From being scared about what others might
think,
From thinking that others will judge me for my
actions

I have come a long way,
From not being able to express myself
From not being able to deal with my emotions,
From not being able to stop depending on others,
I have come a long way,
From not being able to get up from bed…
From not being able to stop being needy,
From not being able to stop pleasing others…
I have come a long way,
I have conquered my inhibitions
I have conquered my fears
I have set boundaries for myself and others…
I have built healthy relationships with myself
and others...

But at times I feel vulnerable
At times there is a reappearance of overthinking
and anxious behaviour…
At times there is a slip but I manage to
recover…
Yes, in my journey of self-discovery,
I have come a long way
I have crossed a bridge,
But I still have the ocean to cross!

I am Queer and I am here

I am Queer and I am here!
I break norms
And have no qualms,
I follow the pattern that my heart desires,
I stretch my wings and land wherever I am
inspired,
I am not necessarily the storm on a turbulent
night,
Nor am I the gentle breeze on a windy night
I am in between the breeze and the storm
I am a woman who refuses to be categorised,
Into the right or left with no mid path in plain
sight,
Do you find it difficult to understand me?
If so, why not ask me?
Than box me as this or that?

Lilies Are Forever

Lilies are forever, they blossom in the spring or
never
But when they spring to life, they leave behind a
mark that never leaves you altogether
Just like my love towards you...
Which will stay forever

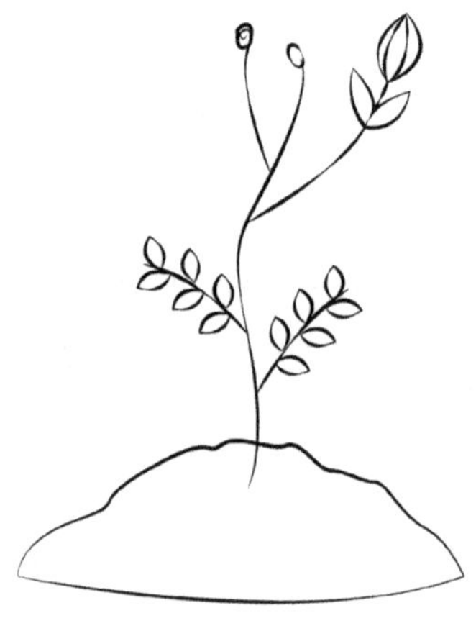

Rain

44

Rain, you drift, you play with the wind...
I hold you, you escape from my fingertips...
You arrive suddenly and fall relentlessly,
I am astounded by your tactful way of bringing
everyone to admire you... by bringing traffic
to a standstill...
Now dear Bangalore rain, please do not laugh at
my few unconnected lines...
I am just like you, not able to connect the entire
city
Drizzling in Jayanagar, but not in Indiranagar
Undecided me, undecided you
So I invite you to a cup of tea on a rooftop cafe
in Bangalore.

Words…

Words, they break you
Words, they make you
Some comfort you ...
Some pierce you...
But you need them and they need you...
Aren't life stories built on a cacophony of
words?
Some word-stories you weave, some life weaves
it for you...
That is why maybe we are taught word-building
when young!
To learn to build our life, through the words that
decide our destiny...

Amma...

Her eyes were watery and face was sweaty, so I
asked her about it...
But she said don't worry, it's nothing...
But the next day, she was right beside me when I
was pacing up and down not having
finished my deadline!

My friend during my best and my worst
A shield from all worries and woes
My sunshine during blistering cold
A cool gal during fun and jokes
She is my Amma and I have known no one like
her ever
There need not be just a day, but everyday is
dedicated to you…

The Piano

I was playing the piano, and I fell asleep
Was it the music that I played? Or the music in
my ear?
Or perhaps it was the symphony that seemed
like a lullaby,
And soothed the child in me …

Sometimes life needs no music

Sometimes life needs no music
Silence is music in itself…
The silence in every pause
The silence in every breath
The silence that resounds in my heart
Whenever I look towards the sky…
Reminding me that I am carefree and me
Life does not always need music
Sometimes, it's the silence that reminds us what
we are…
And what we want to be.

The sky is rosy

The sky is rosy,
A blush tinge of pink, meshing with the milky
blue
Just like your lips darling, drowning in the vast
blue of my eyes
As I devour your face cupped in my arms
With my fingertips tracing the outline of your
face
Wondering how beautiful is your inner self
That it draws me towards every part of your
being
With no conditions, no expectations

Being Held

Being held,
Is something special
Which one should never take for granted
For being contained within, means a sense of
safety
Which some may not be lucky to enjoy,
We are all held by nature, isn't it?
The plants, the earth, the sky?
We forget their presence
For they are omnipresent
But what if they stop playing their role?
The sun stopped shining?
The wind stopped blowing?
The ground stopped holding?
We would all cease to exist
There are many other ways we are held,
By love, by trust, by connection and by care
Let's remember and cherish that we are held
And help hold someone in need
For holding and being held
Is each of our destiny...

I looked at Myself in the Mirror

I looked at myself in the mirror
I was repulsed by the person who stood there
She was someone I struggled to identify with…
I wanted to hit her stomach
Chop her breasts
Why was I like this
That others ridiculed?
I looked at myself in the mirror
I now saw a faint smile
That was trying to catch my eye
I was trying to push back
But the smile was there back again
With a glimmer of hope
That I could not, not see

Imploring me to look within, just one more time

With an open mind, tinted with kindness
Kindness towards self,
I looked at myself in the mirror.
I was now drawn to the person in front of me
Her rawness
Her vulnerability
Her eyes
Her smile
Her imperfectly shaped baggy breasts
Her scarred, protruding stomach
I liked everything about her
But then I was not sure what she liked
We both were not sure, what we liked
So we questioned—what am I?
An Asexual?
A Bisexual?
A Heterosexual?
Or a homosexual?
What do you call a person who is attracted to
self?
Oh, I don't know
I am just a person
Trying to make sense of self…

Being a Single Woman in Bangalore

Bande ond nimisha! (I am coming, one minute)
I told the auto rickshaw driver of namma yatri
Running down the stairs with my stole, and
earphones in hand,
My purse hanging by the side,
I, a single woman in Bangalore, am ready for the
ride…
I pass by signals and stray dogs, seated in the
throne of my auto
Yes! You got it right, I am the auto queen of
Namma Bengaluru
But where am I going you may ask?
I am off to a solo trip to Indiranagar
And yes, from Padmanabhanagar to Indira
Nagar is quite a journey you know!
Hallmarked by bumps and horns and the
in-between traffic jams!

But every now and then, the wind blows through
my hair
Making it all worthwhile,
Even if it's just for a mile.
Whizzing past restaurants and cafes aplenty,
I know some, I don't know some
I smile,
As I calm my inner foodie, that I will visit them
all in good time,
What is so special?
Being a single woman in Bangalore?
You may ask…
Well, from cultural hubs and parks to food hubs
The city has it all!
Last week I was in Cubbon park, reading a book
quietly with legs stretched on a mat and
fellow readers all around

The other week I attended a meet up of like
minded souls
We discussed, we laughed and mulled over our
memories—pleasant and bittersweet
And today I am on my way to a new café
serving street food in town
Chaats, vada pav and some sweet lassi are
something I plan to have…
Don't just let your mouth water, why don't you
take your taste buds on an unforgettable
gastronomical journey?

While I must say it was a great time talking,
But I have to say bye
As the papdi chaat beckons me along with
falooda and some chai…

You should talk to someone

I seek therapy, I said happily
It has increased my awareness and given a better
perspective of the self,
Oh! Why do you need it?
You have friends and family,
And you have everything that you need,
Why do you need to bare your soul to a
stranger?
Only the weak are the ones who complain...
Don't you know?
They questioned me...
I tried to help them understand the benefits of
seeking psychological support, when in
distress,
They pretended to listen, but refused to
understand anything that I said,
I tried in vain, to help them understand,

But failed each time!
When will they realize?
That it is normal to seek help when needed
Without stigma and shame?
When will they stop calling a person weak,
For being brave to talk about their emotions,
With a mental health professional, in a safe
space?
When will they stop viewing everything through
a single lens?
And try to accept everyone with empathy,
And not pity, a person seeking help?

When will they be able to balance their ego,
And understand that they will not become
insignificant,
When I tell them, you need help, you should talk
to someone...